Weird and Wonderful Animals

MARKHORS

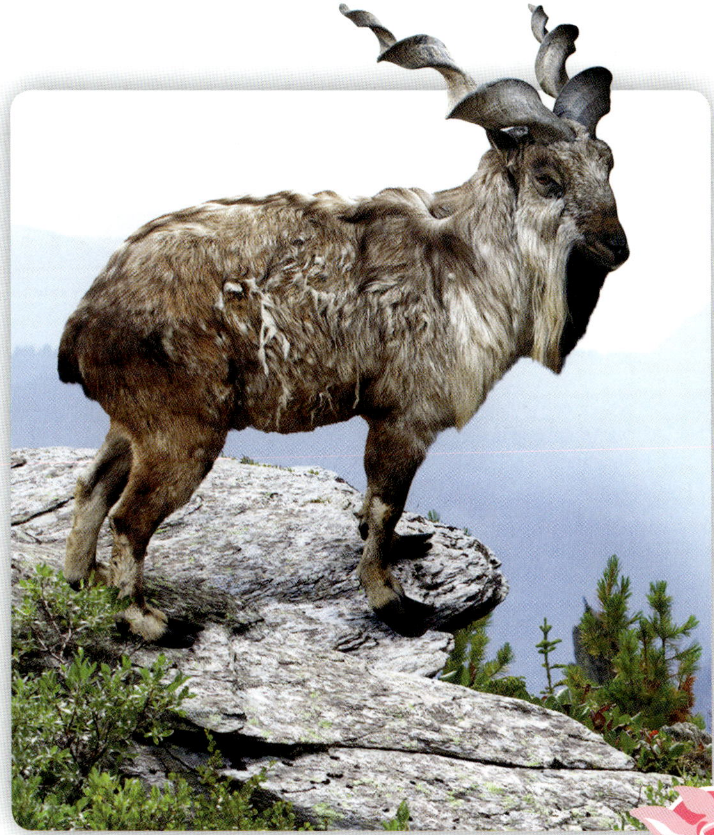

Emma Bassier

DiscoverRoo
An Imprint of Pop!
popbooksonline.com

abdobooks.com

Published by Pop!, a division of ABDO, PO Box 398166, Minneapolis, Minnesota 55439. Copyright © 2020 by POP, LLC. International copyrights reserved in all countries. No part of this book may be reproduced in any form without written permission from the publisher. Pop!™ is a trademark and logo of POP, LLC.

Printed in the United States of America, North Mankato, Minnesota

102019
012020

THIS BOOK CONTAINS RECYCLED MATERIALS

Cover Photo: iStockphoto
Interior Photos: iStockphoto, 1, 5, 6, 8, 11, 12, 13, 14, 15, 16 (right), 17 (top), 17 (bottom), 19, 20, 21, 22, 25, 26–27, 28, 29, 30; Red Line Editorial, 7; Shutterstock Images, 9, 23, 31; Natalia Seliverstova/Sputnik/AP Images, 16 (left)

Editor: Nick Rebman
Series Designer: Jake Slavik

Library of Congress Control Number: 2019942495
Publisher's Cataloging-in-Publication Data

Names: Bassier, Emma, author.

Title: Markhors / by Emma Bassier

Description: Minneapolis, Minnesota : Pop!, 2020 | Series: Weird and wonderful animals | Includes online resources and index.

Identifiers: ISBN 9781532166068 (lib. bdg.) | ISBN 9781644943366 (pbk.) | ISBN 9781532167386 (ebook)

Subjects: LCSH: Wild goats--Juvenile literature. | Capra--Juvenile literature. | Oddities--Juvenile literature. | Mountain goat--Juvenile literature.

Classification: DDC 599.648--dc23

WELCOME TO DiscoverRoo!

Pop open this book and you'll find QR codes loaded with information, so you can learn even more!

Scan this code* and others like it while you read, or visit the website below to make this book pop!

popbooksonline.com/markhors

*Scanning QR codes requires a web-enabled smart device with a QR code reader app and a camera.

TABLE OF CONTENTS

A markhor walks along the side of a mountain. Its hooves click when it moves across the rocks. The animal's brown fur blends in with the surrounding landscape. Enormous horns curl up out of the markhor's head. It puts its head down to **graze**.

Markhors are most active after sunrise and before sunset.

WATCH A VIDEO HERE!

Markhors are wild mountain goats. They are **mammals**. Markhors live in mountainous areas of southern Asia. Most markhors are in Afghanistan and Pakistan.

DID YOU KNOW?

Markhors were likely named for the shape of their horns. In the Pashto language, *mar* means "snake," and *akhur* means "horn."

RANGE MAP

Uzbekistan
Tajikistan
Afghanistan
Pakistan
India
N
W
E
S
Markhor range

A markhor roams its rocky habitat.

Markhors climb steep cliffs. Their **habitat** is high up. The **elevation** ranges from 2,000 to 11,800 feet (600–3,600 m). Some types of trees grow at this height. Oak and pine trees are common.

CHAPTER 2
CORKSCREW HORNS

A markhor's body is up to 6 feet (1.8 m) long. Males weigh approximately 175 to 240 pounds (80–110 kg). Females weigh up to 110 pounds (50 kg). The animal's shaggy fur is usually tan, brown, or black.

LEARN MORE HERE!

Male markhors are much larger than females.

Markhors' horns range in color from dark tan to reddish brown.

A markhor's horns twist out and up from the top of its head. A male's horns can grow up to 5.25 feet (1.6 m) long. Females' horns are much smaller. They are usually only 9 inches (23 cm) long.

DID YOU KNOW?

For some animals, antlers fall off and regrow each year. But a markhor's horns grow for the animal's whole life.

A male markhor shows off his long beard.

Markhors have excellent eyesight.

Their teeth are large and mostly flat.

They also have beards. Males' beards are

longer and thicker than females' beards.

Markhors have **cloven** hooves. Hooves are large, thick toes. Like most hoofed **mammals**, markhors have large bodies and slim legs. Their legs are long and strong.

A markhor's hooves help it walk and climb in rocky areas.

LIFE CYCLE OF A MARKHOR

Mothers have one or two kids at a time.

Females give birth in shallow holes in the ground. A baby markhor is called a kid.

Kids can walk soon after they are born. They travel with their mother. They rely on her milk for up to six months.

Mothers protect their young. Once the kids learn to eat and fend for themselves, they can live on their own.

Markhors live up to 13 years in the wild.

Steep, slippery rocks would cause most animals to fall. But markhors' hooves give them secure holds. The hooves slide into cracks. As a result, markhors can walk on slippery or thin edges. Their long legs

COMPLETE AN ACTIVITY HERE!

A markhor watches for predators from a high ledge.

help them run fast. Their fur keeps them

warm in cold weather.

DID YOU KNOW?

Markhors have thicker fur during the cold winter months. In the summer, their fur becomes thinner.

A markhor spends most of its day eating.

Markhors eat for 12 to 14 hours

every day. They **graze** in the morning

and afternoon. They mostly eat grass.

In the fall and winter, they also eat leaves

and twigs. Markhors grind food with their large, flat teeth.

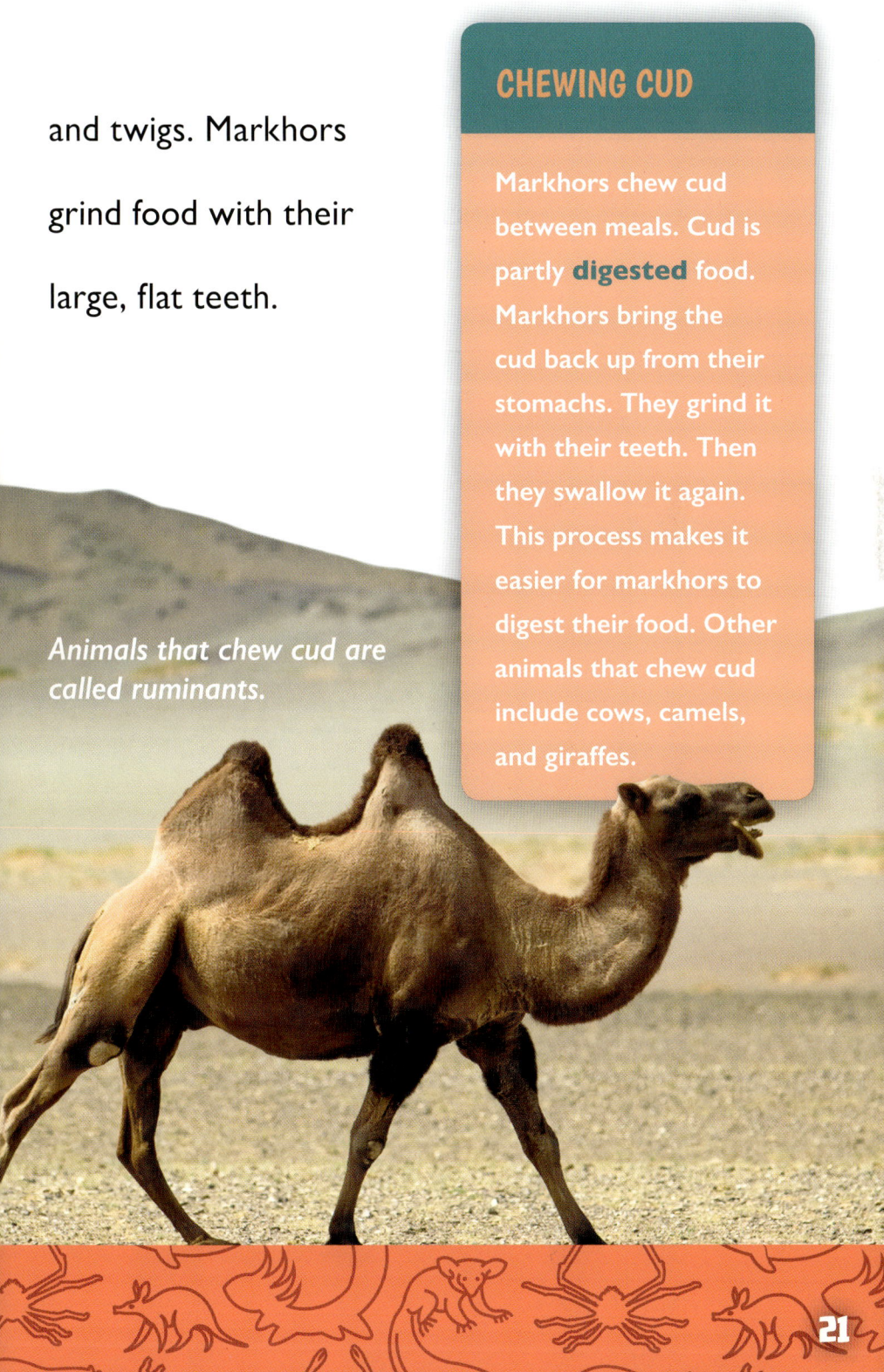

Animals that chew cud are called ruminants.

CHEWING CUD

Markhors chew cud between meals. Cud is partly **digested** food. Markhors bring the cud back up from their stomachs. They grind it with their teeth. Then they swallow it again. This process makes it easier for markhors to digest their food. Other animals that chew cud include cows, camels, and giraffes.

A male markhor walks alone through the mountains.

Females live in herds of eight or nine goats. Males live alone for most of the year. They join herds only when it is time to mate. Markhors mate in the fall and winter. During this time, males fight one another. The winners get to mate.

Two male markhors fight each other using their horns.

CHAPTER 4
SURVIVING THREATS

Markhors use their strong eyesight to spot danger. They look in all directions. Being high up gives them a good view of the surrounding area. Snow leopards are

LEARN MORE HERE!

Markhors are always on the lookout for predators.

their main **predators**. Panthers and

wolves attack them too.

Markhors face several threats.

People hunt them for their horns. Their

habitat is also harmed by people

cutting down trees. In addition, many

markhors live in countries where war

As of 2019, fewer than 6,000 adult markhors lived in the wild.

is common. Wars make it harder for

people to protect these animals.

DID YOU KNOW?

The noise a goat makes is called a bleat.

Markhors use their strong sense of smell to detect predators.

Many people are working to save markhors. They are trying to stop illegal hunting. They are also protecting the

animal's habitat. Saving markhors also

helps snow leopards. The goats are a

main food source for snow leopards.

Markhors are the national animal of Pakistan.

Snow leopards can chase markhors down steep mountains.

MAKING CONNECTIONS

TEXT-TO-SELF

Markhors are a type of goat. Have you ever seen a goat? If so, how was it similar to or different from a markhor?

TEXT-TO-TEXT

Have you read books about another animal that has horns? How does that animal use its horns?

TEXT-TO-WORLD

Markhors face threats. What other animals are in danger? What can people do to help those animals survive?

GLOSSARY

cloven – split into two parts.

digest – to eat food and turn it into energy for the body.

elevation – a measurement of how high a place is above sea level.

graze – to eat grass or other plants in a field.

habitat – the area where an animal normally lives.

mammal – a type of animal that has hair or fur and feeds milk to its young.

predator – an animal that hunts other animals for food.

INDEX

ONLINE RESOURCES

popbooksonline.com

Scan this code* and others like it while you read, or visit the website below to make this book pop!

popbooksonline.com/markhors

*Scanning QR codes requires a web-enabled smart device with a QR code reader app and a camera.